Leaf Litter

Jarod K. Anderson

Published by Crooked Wall Press
Copyright © 2023 Jarod K. Anderson
All rights reserved
ISBN: 9798870221885

Cover Illustration: Maclura pomifera or Osage orange (Maclura
pomifera), Hein Nouwens

Author's Note:

I think of this book as the third in a trilogy, following *Field Guide to the Haunted Forest* and *Love Notes from the Hollow Tree*. The three titles loosely follow a pattern I encounter in my relationship with nature and my own mind. At first, shaken by my own ignorance, I want facts, names, and science. I want a field guide. I want my approach to nature to be "correct." Then, the facts blur and meanings shift. I perceive something more personal in a patch of moss or a Dryad's saddle fungus on a decaying stump. I find love notes in hollow trees. The pattern concludes with something that, at first glance, resembles chaos. I begin to feel overwhelmed by a jumble of past knowledge, fading memory, bygone interests, and the detritus of old priorities and perspectives. Yet, this apparent chaos is not chaos. It's leaf litter. This colorful remainder of past seasons and past selves is not an ending; it's the beginning of new soil and new possibilities. Leaf litter welcomes the next generation of towering oaks. Inevitably, a new spring arrives and something I don't recognize sprouts from the forest floor. I feel like a newcomer once more and the pattern begins anew.

Like the collections that precede it, this book is eclectic, a mix of tones and forms. Somehow, if you're reading this, I suspect you are prepared to embrace my eccentricities. Welcome. I'm sincerely glad you are here.

Jarod K. Anderson
Delaware, Ohio
September 2023

Shapes

One aspect of me
is a forest god,
fox-toothed and stag crowned,
my each pale breath its own season,
meeting the air reborn,
falling solidly to Earth as an oak leaf,
gray as a mourning dove.

Another aspect is an old man,
too tired to step over the curb,
too sad to miss myself.

There are so many of me,
under the narrow canopy of this name,
walking these days that are too small
and still too big to know.

What is there to be done about it?

I refuse to decide,
but I'm eager for friendship in a place as strange as this,
with selves as strange as these.

And strangeness feels friendly to me.

City

That rotting stump,
that pile of yellow leaves,
a city on a golden hill,
remembers what we forget.

The detritivores gather there,
saprobes sharpening their proverbs,
past lives gift new soils,

fungi bundle the words
like warm bread
while moss looks on.

Like all cities,
it's a city of the dead.
Like every life,
it's countless lives as one.

Inkcaps and pinwheels.
Bleeding fairy helmets and mazegills.

Like all lovely things,
you could call it an aftermath,

mourning the tree that was,
once green leaves in tatters,
new growth spent and gone.

Test these thoughts on the city
and hear the gentle hush rebound,
hear a voice among the decay.

All beauty in nature arises from endings.
Seasons and cycles make music from limits.
Forever is a broken measure of success.
Hopelessness lacks imagination.

In the city's cellar,
at home among the dead,
a single seed dreams
of two centuries in sunlight
and even asleep

shivers the dark with potential.

Casting Shadows

We're the sun's magic.

It's tempting to say,
"Ok, but she didn't create us on purpose,"

as if that makes the miracle less worthy.

As if having no need
of mind or intent
disqualifies the project and maker

from reverence.

Bite

My son thinks he's seeing lightning bugs
for the first time.
He's only four and doesn't remember last July.
"Don't try to grab them," I say.
"Hold your hand like this."
We stand by the cemetery fence.
I show him how to raise his palm up beneath them,
a pink platform floating up through the dark.
"These are big dipper fireflies. They dip. They swoop."
I draw a "J" in the air.
"So, we catch them from below."
He lands one, too hard, and laughs.
"Gentle. Don't grab. Just watch."
The little beetle turns a half circle and flies off.
"Can I keep one?"
"No. We don't keep. We only visit."
Out across the cemetery,
they are shining green and yellow on the graves.
We are growing old.
The Earth.
The nation.
The village of ghosts I call myself.
"Do they bite, Dada?"
"No, sweetheart."
Not in the way you mean.
Not in the way you mean.

Late

For most of the history of life on Earth,
and life on land specifically,
flowers did not exist.

It's hard to imagine the landscape without flowers,
without the marriage of blooms and bees.
Yet, their long absence feels hopeful.

Flowers teach a lesson through absence,
a lesson that nature is never too old to learn new tricks,
to redefine and reimagine.

Every blossom's long road to existence reminds us
that life is a verb, a process,
an unfolding story of awakenings.

What new wonders are on the way to this world?
What strange hope is budding down in the rich soil of fallen years.

Close

Monsters don't hide under your bed
because they want to "get you."

If you're reading this,
you may notice that they never "get you."

They do it to feel togetherness.
They do it because their time in this world is limited,
so they choose a place that matters.

A place close to you.

Leaf Litter

Today is a hard one.
I'm failing to shower.
To eat. To do. Anything.

I feel the weight of what's
beneath my bed.
The untuned mandolin.
The knotted jump rope.
The worksheets from therapy.
The books I almost read.

I picture a dumbbell,
a skiff's shattered hull
on a dust-bunny seabed.

All these things were once me,
discarded but for their hunger
for my space and thoughts.

What are they now?

My depression says, "defeats,"
red ink on my permanent record,
a dragon's horde of wasted hours.

But I see the woods beyond my window
and they say something different.

Leaf litter on the forest floor,
slowly becoming soil,
does not represent the failure
of past summers' trees.

It is the process by which the past
nourishes the present and future.

The same is true for my old selves,
my bygone passions,
last season's interests.

Maybe I can't shower today,
but I can sense a choice,
a fork in the path.

I will choose the trees.
I will be thankful for the leaf litter and,
with an eye toward new, green shoots,
will await a shift in the weather.

Local Color

When the wind blows,
that old lantern sways on its hook,
answering the crickets with the tuneless whine of fretting metal.

That's when all the shadows bend and reach,
haunting that old, covered bridge.
Peeled paint breathing like a reef.

There's nothing on the other side.
Thickets and thorn-wounds.
A dirt road too dead for weeds.

Lighting the way is a paradox,
somehow making us all less safe
with a lie of knowability.

Folks ask, "who keeps that old lantern lit?"

I ask, "who'd dare to put it out?"

Life is a Poem

It doesn't give us everything.
Just some things.

Two sturdy branches.
A basket of dawns.

If we stitch our web there,
and the morning strings it with dew,

the beauty isn't a gift.
It's a partnership.

Because life, like poetry,
means only what we let it mean.

Around the Corners

People think the minotaur is just the monster,
those blunt teeth as big as birthday cards
dividing you like smoke.

Suicide is a permanent solution to a temporary problem.
Depression is like a disease, just less reputable.

They forget what else the minotaur is.
It's that big animal smell in the dark, fur and breath and shit whispering,
"it's true, it's all true, I'm here and I'm hungry."

Self-harm is illogical. Take a minute. Just think it out.
Get the thoughts down on paper.

You know that bull-head has chosen a long corridor to watch,
that it waits for movement, tense as a rattlesnake,
all light-starved muscle and potential energy.

Have you read that book I recommended?
It's free online.

That punished and cursed thing is the reason that, no, you can't just go
in with a headlamp and graph paper.
If you'd been there, you'd know.
The dirt is clotted with easy answers and old blood.

Have you tried yoga?
Meditation?

There are children running on the stones.
Your memories are ghosts
and the house they haunt is you.

I used to be sad sometimes,
then I chose to be happy.

Focus too much on the monster
and the maze will sweep you away like a riptide.
Don't, and feel your fear peeling open eyes on the back of your skull.

Are you getting enough sunshine?
It could be a vitamin issue.

I strain to hear the minotaur running
and know I've missed something essential.
Does it have hooves or feet?

Are those scars from a cat?
Do you own a cat?

How can something I think of every day
always stay half a myth?

Scale

The truth is,

from lunar orbitals to electron orbitals,
we can always find a scale on which
we are powerless.

We can also find a scale on which
we are powerful.

The universe is nested stories,
grand and intimate,
spinning like clockwork, like dancers.

We do not steer the planets,
but when we come home to our own contexts,

there is no doubt we are titans.

Raccoon Facts #1

Raccoons evolved hands
just so they could refuse to shake yours.

High-fives also aren't happening.

Being a Fool

I can identify every species of bird I encounter
except the ones I don't know.

They never notice.

Only the blue jays call me by name,
and it always sounds like scolding.

"Jay-red! Jay-red!" shivering the dogwoods.

You need knowledge of species names to enjoy nature

like a raccoon needs a
dinner napkin.

Don't meet the wild to feel smart.

Meet her to fall in love.

Oh Well

Somewhere between denial
and surrender
is, *oh well.*

I hurt today.
Oh well.

I'm going for a walk and if it doesn't help,
oh well.

I'm not going to panic-buy anything.
I'm not going to harm myself in frantic flight to distraction.

I'm going to take pride in every heartbeat
I can hold my pain gentle and inert.

Oh well.
My quiet victory.

Oh well acknowledges the disappointment
without meeting its demands,
without handing it the keys.

Next time you skin both knees
falling short of your hopes,

try, *oh well.*

It's not a celebration of defeat,
but it is a celebration,
a farewell party for a hurt exiting our present moment,
a whispered thanks that we can endure.

Because

I don't know why it feels so good to touch a tree.
Maybe because our hands evolved to grasp them.
Maybe because the life within is so different from ours
and exactly the same.
Maybe because it's like touching time,
touching soil and sun and seasons of rain.
Maybe our lungs know what we owe them.
Maybe trees are knotholes to memory,
through them we clasp our own grass-stained fingers.
Maybe it's utility —fire, shade, and shelter.
Maybe our ancestors linger in the branches,
smiling kindly at our lovely, silly lives.
Maybe not knowing is the soul of the magic.
Maybe because it's love.

Crisis

There's a bear circling.
He's not your enemy.
He doesn't hate you,
but he will chew your naked throat
if that's what the hour demands.

We seldom admit the seductive comfort of hopelessness.
It saves us from ambiguity.
It has an answer for every question:
"There's just no point."
Hope, on the other hand, is messy.
It's a burning branch that stings our eyes.
If it might all work out, then we have things to do.
We must weather the possibility of happiness.

There's a bear circling.
He does not wish us harm.
His stomach is empty but for heat
and rising thunder.
He is not in charge of our welfare.

We are.

Nostalgia

There will come a time when these days
are the good old days.
This will be wrong.
It is always wrong to imagine
an unstained past.

Present work is rarely charming
to those who sweat over it,
and somehow,
it's always easier to think we missed our chance
to love this world.

To save it.

Grove

My heart is a hemlock grove.

Loving is not the growl of a chainsaw.
It does not strip lumber from my shaded hills.

It is not a thoughtless harvest.

Loving does not deplete the land.
It nourishes it.

To love is to plant a tree.
As it grows, I grow.

Soft and new and evergreen.

Spinning Wheel

There's a wheel in the rain

that spins clouds into long strands of river.

Fingers of land knit the flow
into seas that clothe the Earth.

This deep gown,
stitched with leaping fish and whale song,
catches the sun's eye,

each glance a new cloud.

There's a wheel in the rain.

Breadwinner

Each breath is a meal.
Fifteen times a minute.
With or without thought.

Food direct from the forest.
From the sea.
No need for plate nor fork nor flame.

A cellular hunger,
the appetite of our blood,
raw and wild and vital.

Think of what feeds us most.
At whose table do we sit?

Ruin

We want to call it quits when we are certain.
Certainty seems sweeter than not knowing.

It's too late.
We're too broken.
The game is already over.

Hopelessness loves to masquerade as wisdom
and is so much easier to befriend.

Until it isn't.

The future is a big place.
Resist dismissing it with small words.

End the sentence. The paragraph. The page.

But do not close the book.

Scare

We know that crows are very intelligent.

The fact that scarecrows frighten them,
stuffed shirts and stitched frowns,

suggests there's something we don't know
about scarecrows.

Bone Collector

A vulture reads a poem in the bones,
sensing what we tend to forget.

Deer skulls like ghost ships
sailing the leaf litter are beautiful.

Rotting logs with capes of moss
and mushroom crowns bleed magic.

A ribcage cathedral in the stream
braids hymns from water and light.

We couple loveliness with growth,
but decay is not just approaching absence.

Death also blooms.

Not a Mistake

It's not a mistake to need rest.
Or seek help.
Or make secret pacts with household spiders.
Or find friendship in the dark beneath a log.
Or to think "hello" into the night sky and wait for a response.
Or sink your fingers into the soil to see if they take root.
Or, despite everything, to love this world.

Legendary

Acknowledge the monsters you defy,
the storms you weather.
Name them.

Tooth-breaker. Heart-biter.
Medical debt. Age and pain.

There are those walking this earth
to whom your life would seem a bare rock
rising from angry seas.

Hate's-fang. Winter's voice.
Lost friends. Abuse and regret.

Yet, there you are,
stringing together days like flowers in your crown.
Respect your own vital splendor.

Wounded,
breath freezing into story-hall smoke,
and very much alive.

Sip

A mosquito drank from my hand
and I left her to it.

She departed swollen, cherry-red,
into the summer dark.

"Now much of you is me," I said.

Carry us from dim capillaries
out to the galaxy of moth and moon.

Know me, August evening.
My crimson words on borrowed wings.

"Thank you."

Brave

Every kind of love is terrifying
because all love is a sort of fusion,
a way of mingling.

Through love,
we infuse a person or idea
with a bit of ourselves and desperately hope
they treat it kindly,
because it has left our control.

It has stopped being me
and started being us.

Sincerity feels frightening because it is powerful.

Irony and detachment feel less frightening
because they are

less.

Bespoke

Butterfly wings and grizzly bear jaws
are both successful pathways to survival.

There is no single, best way to thrive.

Gasp

Every gray day I inhale pain
and exhale poetry.

It doesn't matter that I don't have enough
breath in me to turn the whole sky to song.

What matters is that I know this
and try anyway.

Because if I can't shatter the jaw of heartache on Earth,
I still won't shake its fucking hand.

Challenge

Challenge your own guilt
about things you do not control.

Tell it to hush.

No one chooses exhaustion or despair.
No one chooses pain or abuse.
No one chooses anxiety or illness.

You didn't invite these things
and they don't define you,

but I am so proud of you for enduring them.

Crown

There are moments when hardship
welcomes me home to my power.

Like walking through bitter cold and rain.
Like sleepless sadness.

When I take it all in and think,
"here is a hard world and here am I,
the creature who may walk this place at will."

Generous woe.
For making me magnificent

Messy Desk

When existence seems absurd,
ask yourself what is out of step,
reality or your expectations
of control and permanence.

Who told you this would last,
that your power was forever,
and the hands at your command
are this world's defining miracle.

They sold you these ideas
as if they were treasures,
great relics of purpose and dignity,
but these burdens neither teach nor heal.

Poetry needs concrete images to resonate,
but today I have none to offer.
There is one, dusty cheerio beneath my monitor
and it stubbornly refuses to be poetic.

I can empathize.
I can also carry on anyway.
Hope, like that cheerio, may also be stubborn.

We are special and small.
We are real and finite.
We are good in defiance of perfect.

Our choices matter most when made
with honest acceptance.

Yes, one day we'll be dust and echoes.
Yet, how incredible it is that today
we are not.

Four

My favorite bread recipe has four ingredients.
Water. Flour. Salt. Yeast.
When the loaf is ready, I think,
"this seems like magic."

Seems?

I recall,
of course simple things produce magic.
I have internalized too much of the marketing fiction
that worth requires complexity.

.

Raccoon Facts #2

In literal terms,
Virginia opossums have more teeth than raccoons.

In figurative terms,
raccoons have far more teeth.

There's a reason we reach for metaphor
when fact and truth part ways.

Whale Fall

Sip tea by the morning glories,
taste leaf and light and steam,
warm on unhurried lips,
and think, *this is our Earth.*

But send one thought away.
Send it on an errand, down deep
to the whale fall.

You know it's there,
even now while you breathe air
and fold your soft hands in sunlight.

Where midnight is a place
they are building a cathedral in reverse,

singing in the ribcage sanctuary,
a slow hymn of tooth and claw,
chewing the arches back to earth.

Far from your teacup,
in a boom-and-bust town
of sleeper shark and spider crab,

you will sense a homecoming
hanging in the heavy dark,
where one great heartbeat became many,
became words scattered on sand,

this is our Earth.

The whale is not here.
The whale is not gone.
Like her mother's milk.
Like your tea.
Your morning.

The years before your birth.
The ecosystems you are
and the ones you will become.

The mystery of it all
is both the ghost that hunts the hall
and the steam rising from your tea,
bending with each sigh,
intimate and out of reach.

The ground knows what you suspect,
that there is an unbroken path
from where you sit
to leviathan bones.

Feel it like a scar beneath your feet,
leading down to where the whale
called her congregation
from black water.

May it haunt without menace.

Not because it is powerless,
but because it is yours to share.

This is our Earth.

Honors

To feel the sun on your shoulders
is to touch the driving force of all life on Earth,
ancient and profound.

To breathe is to converse
with forests and seas, vast and green,
intimate as "I love you."

When you weigh your accomplishments,
start here.

You were born with the highest honors
our world can give.

As we age, praise from our mothers
can feel like it "doesn't count."

It counts. It counts. It counts.

Likes

How much of your life is spent in the service of connection?
Describing how you feel.
Who you are.
Making art.
Telling stories.

How long do you spend online scribbling notes slipped across the planet?

Look at how we live.
How we spend our hours.
It may feel grim and addictive,
but sus out the root cause.

We are all endlessly falling in love with one another.

Hiker's Paradox

Something about walking along the simple symmetry
of an orderly street makes life feel complicated.

Something about walking among the complex tangle
of a wild woodland makes life feel simple.

It's almost as if making our spaces efficient
is not always the same as making them good to inhabit.

Not Okay

I am not okay today.
So, in the absence of okay,
what else can I be?

I can be gentle.
I can be unashamed.
I can turn my pain into connection.
I can be a student of stillness.
I can be awake to nature.
I can sharpen my empathy
against the stone of my discomfort.

I am not okay,
but I am many worthy things.

Phase

It's worth remembering that if ghosts are real,
then you already are one.

In 1,000 years you'll be dancing in churchyard rain
on some shaggy hillside
and you'll think of the body you once had
as a strange, short phase.

Like a bad haircut.

Tune

Consciousness is a kind of music that, one day,
the universe began humming to itself.

We ask "why?"

But we know the answer
because we have sung to empty kitchens
while doing the dishes.

There are kinds of silence that are pure potential,
that are beauty demanding to be born.

Win Condition

Life isn't a game.
It's walking a pinewood path
collecting stones.
You won't win or lose.
There will be no single rock,
heavy as silence,
that crowns you worthy
of your heartbeat.

That crown sprouts
like antlers from your skull
when you ask Earth to take root
in your bones,
when you smile kindly
at the ache in your chest,
when you turn away from victory
and walk toward gratitude.

Ornithology Abridged

Hummingbirds:
I shall sip nectar from this flower in a silent ballet.

Woodpeckers:
I'MMA STAB THE BUGS OUTTA THIS TREE WITH MY FACE-KNIFE!!!

Bare

Why do we associate skeletons
with autumn and Halloween?
It's simple.
Some people, like trees, are deciduous,
shedding all their flesh in the Fall
only to regrow it again in the spring.
A strong wind and suddenly you are bare bones
standing in the pale, October sunlight.

Drab

Peace is a technology and a discipline.
Like agriculture.
Like medicine.

There's nothing sexy about it.
Like spreading manure.
Like hospital hygiene.

It's boring and needy,
demanding patience and endless compromise,
compromise, compromise.

Hateful compromise.

Robbing our feeling of righteousness.
A gray drizzle on the blaze
of holy indignation.

It doesn't sell tickets.
It doesn't build ego.
It doesn't heat the blood with national pride.

All it does is keep a child with pink shoes alive
long enough to eat breakfast.

All it does is stop one wide-eyed toddler
from trying to wake his mother's corpse

Mammalian

Bats call out and listen to the shape of the world.
Echolocation.
Wing-fingers reaching,
finding the dark sky reaching back,
helpful hands gently pulling.
Onward.

Whales call out and listen to the shape of the world.
Biosonar.
Fin-fingers reaching,
finding the vast sea reaching back,
helpful hands gently pulling.
Onward.

Humans call out and listen to the shape of the world.
Community.
Needful fingers reaching,
finding new family reaching back,
helpful hands gently pulling.
Onward.

Teeth

Nature is a comfort.
A teacher.

A still meadow humming
in a voice of bumblebees may center us
when we're adrift.

But, recall,
the badger is also nature.
The bear. The wolf. The mantis.

How do we answer injustice?

Sometimes the bee's meadow must remind trampling feet
that it also conceals teeth.

Perceive

You can perceive energy in the air.
(Temperature)
You can perceive shifts in the atmosphere.
(Wind)
You can perceive beyond what is,
to what may be.
(Imagination)
But can you penetrate the fog of familiarity
and perceive yourself as a true wonder
of the natural world?
(Insight)

Pre-Date Questionnaire:

How many quarter-full water glasses are on your desk?

Do you ever check under your bed for monsters?

What's your first move if you awaken as a new ghost?

How often do you test yourself for telekinesis?

Do you talk to trees?

What would child-you be most proud of about adult-you?

How did you care for someone else this week?

Have you ever helped a turtle across the road?

How much does happiness factor into your idea of success?

How dependent upon money is your idea of happiness?

If you could transform into a walrus, when and why would you?

Which smell is a gateway to a cherished memory?

If you could wish away one daily chore, which would you choose?

What is your definition of family?

Blanket fort or treehouse?

Maintenance Man

I am endlessly broken and
endlessly repaired.
One handcrafted scar.
A Ship of Theseus.

My rust-bitten life,
shattered, patched, replaced,
without pause.

Some days,
it feels like growth
to give up on being whole.
To stop being the thing,

and start being the worker,
the soul within the task,
knuckle split from a slipped wrench,
black crescents beneath my nails.

Not the engine,
but the reason it still growls
like a winter-starved dog.

One more day.

Starting Place

Your personal sense of peace
does not require you to first assess the character of your nation,
the health of your planet,
or even your own future.

Whatever your broader hopes and goals,
you will need to cultivate a garden of calm, pleasant moments
to nourish you on the path ahead.

It is appropriately difficult to overlook the evil in this world.

It is dangerously easy to overlook the good.

Skein

She loops and knots the yarn,

saying it's a spell to change time
into a thing we can hold,
a way to keep her loves warm.

Crochet is her offering to a mind
with teeth that never stop growing,
thoughts that must chew and chew.

She wears button-up pajamas,

like a kid on a Christmas card,
cross-legged on our battered couch,
TikTok buzzing on her thigh.

Her skein paces the rug
while twists of twilight wool
are hooked into warmer winters.

I sit beside her and feel the magic,

feel the years tugged into shape,
my too-thin memory of gentle evenings
changing beneath her fingers

into something I can hold.

Failed Poem About the Moon

I try and fail to photograph the moon.
Yet, she speaks through my failure.
She says,
"You can't save me for later."
"You can't post me online."
"You can't press me between pages."
"Be here. Right now. With me."
"I won't accept anything less."

Coming Up for Air

A fist-sized stone
deep in the Earth
is on the edge of becoming magma.

It has been underground
for billions of years,
in darkness since before life awoke.

It will rise,
touch sunlight,
taste rain and cool,
erode into soil,
become new, green grass,
nourish a mother deer,
be born into a wildflower meadow.

The stone will take its first breath.

Counting

I spent lifetimes trying to count the stars.
I failed, but if I could go back,
I wouldn't do a thing differently.

It's not that I couldn't count stars.
It's that I couldn't count them all.

I spent lifetimes trying to count the stars.
I succeeded when I realized
I wouldn't do a thing differently.

Synthesis

The mother tree builds the seed,
until the moment when the seed builds itself.

It's the same with spirituality.
With art, philosophy, and writing.

At first, we all must borrow,
calling on another's momentum to be our own,
inheriting the nutrients we need to grow.

Then, we surprise ourselves.

And we begin to trust our own meaning.
And we begin to sense our own style.
And we begin to honor our own perspective.
And we begin to find our own voice.

The seed takes root,
building something familiar

and entirely new.

Not an Owl

I am not an owl.
But I can appreciate owlness
in a way the owl cannot.

Because I do know what it is
to not be an owl.
No night vision.
No silent flight
through the lattice of sugar maple
and shagbark hickory.

Often, we cannot sense the presence
of our own magic.

It is a worthy practice to sense it in others.

Tidy

Do not mourn your messy past.
A uniform slab of concrete is tidy,
but nothing grows there.

A Few Hours

Yesterday,
I spent a few hours as a volunteer,
working with a team,
planting white oaks in a young woodland
at Stratford Ecological Center.

We dug holes,
sweating among the mayapples and spring beauties,
smiling at ramps and rumors of morels,
plucking out honeysuckle and garlic mustard,
comparing notes on gardening.

Today,
my back is stiff,
but the feeling fades by lunch.
I move on. On to buy the bread.
On to the thing after that.

We sank roots,
joined by a mutual goal.
The people and the trees.
Anchored in camaraderie.
Anchored in fertile soil.

A century from now,
ten dozen oaks feed and shelter an ecosystem,
rising eighty feet from a single afternoon,
from a few hours of communal effort,
from a broader definition of community.

Buyer's Remorse

If you spend away your humanity
in order to buy your safety,

you may one day be surprised to discover

that safety is not a currency
that can buy back your humanity.

Pond

Half the cells in our bodies belong to other species.
Our skin warms wild yeast and mites.

Most of our substance is water,
passing through on a cycle of sea and sky.

Next time you pass a woodland pond,
offer a "hello cousin,"

and grin at your literal and figurative reflection.

Raccoon Facts #3

Raccoons have a language
that is 70% curse words.

Humans never hear the remaining 30%.

The Long View

A boot may crush a lily,
but lilies will remain long after
that boot is worn to dust.

Boots neither sprout nor root.

We may be trampled by sorrows,
but we are more lily than boot
and nature waits and whispers,

"grow and thrive again."

2AM

I am crying tonight.
Not bad tears.
Just "I am here" tears.
Like dew or clover.
Elk or snowmelt.
I am here.

I didn't expect to cry.
Or to be here.
After 2AM.
Tonight or ever.

But I am.
Here.
Crying.
For dew or clover.
Elk or snowmelt.
Here and unexpected.
Loved.
Loved.
Loved.

Afterlife

What if he let the ghosts write this one?

What if the poet is dreaming of lichen
on an old boundary stone,
leaving his desk unguarded
while spectral fingers pluck synapses
like spider's silk?

What if he pretends it was his idea,
dozing in the clover while autumn
strips the mulberry trees
and pelts the shed with walnuts,

keys tapping in an empty room?

What if it's a smuggling operation,
secrets tucked into a knothole
calling out for grass-stained denim
and curious peerings?

What if it's all about thought?
What if brains aren't what you think?
What if intention misses the point?

What if nature treats personhood
with the same respect as fallen wood
and flowing water?

Preserving. Reimagining.

What if heron-print texts
on muddy riverbeds are holy books
even without a reader,
without a writer?

What if we remind you

that eyes do not bring light into the world,
that they just interpret it?

What if people are the same?

What if we don't conjure consciousness,
only borrow it,

an otter dreaming on a seafoam bed,
a falcon riding warm air upward,
a human sensing self in the swirl of leaf litter?

What would that mean for the long ages
when you have no body?

Does sunshine depend on vision to be real?

Do those with sight know more of light
than moss on splintered stone?

What if we told you a brain is just a keyhole
through which all the universe looks on hold,
looks expectant for the coming key?

What if that key matters less than you suppose?

What if, when you pass the door, you will not be the same,
but that too is kinder than you imagine,
kind as seasons and sleep and sudden morning?

What if the poet awakens uncertain,
stiff-necked with his nose to the ground,
leaves in his beard,
thinking the soil smells of coming mushrooms,
dismissing the scent as unscientific?

70

What if the truest statements must remain ajar,
must linger on as questions,
stifled laughs beneath the floorboards,

or betray the natural generosity of not knowing?

Scratch Pad

- Why is grief so hungry all the time?
  And why can't it ever decide what it wants to eat?

- Humans calling themselves "outside nature" is like a child declaring themselves "a runaway" from a tent in the kitchen.

- Leaving my house to walk in the woods feels like missing someone deeply, then realizing they've been waiting in the next room the entire time.

- Any creative act, even if its core message is "to hell with all this," is a hopeful declaration that what we are all doing here together is a worthy endeavor.

- We must teach meaning-making as an empowering skill. We must reject the search for meaning as a haunting imperative.

- I feel confident that moss and fire are cousins.
  I also feel confident that I cannot explain why.

- Creativity is nourished by play. If it's possible to fail doing it, then it doesn't count as play.

- Cultivating gratitude is self-care.

- Anyone else ever get the odd feeling they are missing someone they haven't met yet? Like nostalgia aimed at an unknown future rather than an unreachable past.

Making Space

I often walk the woods alone.

Not because I crave solitude for solitude's sake,
but because when I am the only human
it is much easier to notice

other kinds of companionship.

Fifth Grade

I wish I could tell 10-year-old me that you're doing it all wrong
and that is correct.

That there is no way to be too good for danger. Or pain. Or sadness.

That uncertainty is not a character flaw.

That the search for meaning isn't a clock ticking down to "too late."

That numbness is more prison than shelter.

That when you mourn a fallen wren or a wind-split tree,
you're on the right track.

Unerring

However you manage to be at peace today
is correct.

It doesn't matter that the laundry is still piled
on the chair.

That dragon will keep your victory safe for you
until you claim it.

What matters is that you found peace today.

Memory is as fickle as fire and burns as it warms,
but risk its services anyway.

Ask it to show you a day when you did not find peace,
and by its flickering light,

see the shape of your present triumph.

Do not pester that triumph with petty questions
about petty details.

However you manage to be at peace today
is correct.

Is more than correct.

Is spectacular.

Mourning Tree

I once heard the Osage-orange called,
"The tree that mourns the mammoth."
A widowed species lost in memory.

The knobby, green fruit,
meant for eating, for seed distribution,
rots in the sun like cut lilies on a grave.

Ecosystems do not mourn with words.
They mourn with bone and bough.
Extinction is an empty place at the table.

The mammoth is not coming to dinner,
but humans, squirrels and bobwhite try to fill in,
cultivating new generations of trees.

Saplings wake in a time of absent friends,
and in ten Septembers' growth,
drop fruit 10,000 years out of season.

Sun Song

Once,
A little girl heard cicadas for the first time.
She asked, "is that the sound the sun makes?"

And, of course, the answer is, "no."
And, of course, the answer is, "yes."

The sun speaks many languages.

Come Home

When in doubt,
come home to you.
To now.
Become an acolyte of what's within reach.
Of forgiveness.
Of your desk drawer.
Of feeling each breath.
There will always be problems too big for you.
An unknown future.
A tragic world.
That's ok.
Just be you.
You're the world too.
Refocus.
Come home.

Notes:

"Whale Fall," "Afterlife," and "City" originally appeared in *Atmos* (Nov 2023)

"Around the Corners" originally appeared in *Nightmare Magazine* (Aug 2022)

Acknowledgements:

Thank you to my partner, editor, designer, and favorite poet, Leslie J. Anderson. I couldn't do this without you.

Thank you to my son Arthur for helping me see nature with a newcomer's eyes.

Thank you to Sarah Sykes, Rhiannon Riehl, Alex McCue, and Amy Butcher for helping to shape this collection with your feedback and encouragement.

More Books by Jarod K. Anderson

Poetry:

Field Guide to the Haunted Forest (2020)
Love Notes from the Hollow Tree (2022)

Nonfiction:

Something in the Woods Loves You (2024 Timber Press/
Hachette)

Author Website: jarodkanderson.com

Podcast Website: CryptoNaturalist.com

Support: Patreon.com/CryptoNaturalist

X: @CryptoNature

Facebook: /CryptoNaturalist

Instagram: @CryptoNaturalist

Made in the USA
Middletown, DE
04 September 2024

60345602R00046